In the beginning...

A young boy. A little chubby. Wears his black hair in a flattop.

He loves baseball and his collie dog, Tippy. He and Tippy wander the fields and woods behind the small brick home where his family lives. He, his older sister and brother, plus his loving parents, share the same small house in a tiny, ancient farming town, barely a dot on the county map.

That lonely little boy was me.

Growing up in rural Maryland, the most popular public place was the old wooden dime store where I woofed down more than my share of penny candy. The proprietor was an ancient man whose family had been the founders of the town of Clarksburg, our home. In reality, all there was to Clarksburg was Barr's grocery, a somewhat embellished title for a dime store, an elementary school, an old Baptist church and an old-style gas station, with 1940's era gas pumps. Route 355 bisected the town and carried the weary traveler from Gaithersburg in the south, to Damascus in the north.

At the top of the hill on route 355, there was an historical marker, a large rock with a plaque that commemorated a civil war skirmish that occurred in a tavern that used to stand on that spot. I used to haul my trusty toy rifle up that hill, hide behind the

1

large rock, and pretend to shoot at cars as they drove by on route 355. Today, that would be a dangerous pastime considering the proliferation of gun violence in America.

Clarksburg was the kind of town that requires a boy to develop a strong sense of make-believe and Tippy and I spent many hours exploring the corn fields behind the house, carrying my trusty toy rifle, tracking a variety of imagined "bad guys". With no large buildings to impose on the rural sky, I grew up with a sense of a wide expanse of heaven bordered only by fleecy clouds and mature forests. This, of course, was years before air pollution invaded the atmosphere of our bucolic home environment.

My parents both worked for the Federal Government. They commuted the thirty-five miles from Clarksburg into Washington DC. Eventually the drive got to be too much for them and they began searching for a house closer to their government workplaces.

This heralded the first major change in my life, and the precursor to the actual topic of this story.

We moved into Bethesda, Maryland. In the 1950's Bethesda was a sleepy suburb that had not yet exploded into the metropolitan center of tall buildings and heavy traffic that it is today. We moved into a newly-built house in a quiet suburban neighborhood. There were still a fair number of trees and our street ended two blocks from our new house. I discovered fodder for my imagination while exploring the "wilds" that started just two blocks from home. New homes were being built and there was only a dirt road that wandered thru the construction zone for almost a mile. I can still recall the smell of new wood that surrounded me as I explored the interiors of new houses being built. Tippy and I had found a new "place". Sadly, Tippy was aging as I was growing up. She died one night while I was alone with her and my parents were at choir practice.

I never forgave them.

How could my life ever be the same?

In 1957, Jerry Lee Lewis released "Whole Lotta Shakin'". I saw him perform the rock 'n roll classic on the Ed Sullivan Show one Sunday night. As you undoubtedly know, a string of rockers destined for rock stardom appeared on that show over the years. For thousands, probably even millions of early teen kids, those appearances on Ed Sullivan were nothing short of life-changing.

Nothing would be quite the same afterward...

The Ed Sullivan experience clearly marked my explosive introduction to rock 'n roll. That evening, when I was just ten, swung the weathervane of my life into a completely new direction.

Oh, I would still live for baseball right thru junior high and high school, but my heart cried out for the Rolling Stones and, eventually, on formative Sunday nights on the Ed Sullivan Show, I, along with an entire generation searching for redemption, encountered The Beatles, Chuck Berry, Elvis, The Rolling Stones, James Brown...and so very many more.

My God! How could my life ever be the same?

I knew that I had to grow my hair and reimagine my church-based musical training in the service of Rock 'n Roll! But my passion for rock n' roll music, and the mechanism that slowly but completely re-oriented my life, took years to mature. After all, when I first glimpsed Elvis, I was still only twelve years old and hadn't yet discovered girls. By the time I reached junior high school, the seed implanted by those nights viewing the rock 'n roll legends, had started to grow.

Suddenly, I had a girlfriend. Her name was Kim and she was blessed with incredible physical attributes. Not that I vaguely knew how to respond to her smoldering persona, but my body responded long before my mind. As we waited for my afternoon school bus home, she had a way of leaning against my back as I waited in the cafeteria. The feelings I experienced were new and powerful and when my bus arrived, I usually had to cover the bulge of my pants with my notebook!

By high school, my war between sex and sports became heated. Baseball was my god. I worshipped daily in service to my high school team. But sex was coming up fast. (Pardon the pun).

Still, religion was the anchor to my growing sexual speedboat. Somehow, I got thru high school without any paternity suits, but the hormones were whispering "Wait until college…"

By the time I reached the University of Maryland, I had exorcised the demon of the crewcut. Throughout high school, my hair had been worn in a "crewcut". It was simply how baseball players wore their hair. My high school baseball coach would have had a heart attack if he could have seen today's pro players with long hair and beards.

At any rate, I had undertaken the task of growing my hair longer. What I discovered was that my hair had become so used to sticking up in a crewcut, that when it was allowed to grow beyond the normal bounds of a crewcut, it simply continued to grow vertically! It wasn't long before I had a three-inch thatch of hair pointing straight up and out. Nightly, I indevoured to smash it down on the front and empty sides of my head. But the hair was having none of that. As surely as I pressed it down, it shot back up.

I finally consulted my mother, who recommended "straightening" my hair. I agreed and a week later, I had what looked like a "bowl cut" - the straightened hairs simply fell down over my eyes and ears. The crewcut was gone for good. Suddenly, I had a hairstyle! It was a change that would alter my life forever.

Looking back, hair was charged with social baggage for an entire generation. When my hair reached the length of about fourteen inches, I became a target for ridicule and violence at college. "The jocks" and the frat boys were still entrenched in the short hair mindset. On campus, they pursued me to my classes, shouting and occasionally throwing rocks. To me, my hair was worth it. I had crossed an invisible line as real as the Grand Canyon. I had become a "hippie". I protested the war in Vietnam, I marched for liberal causes, I even joined the Students for a Democratic Society (the fabled SDS!) During my college career, I lived at home to save money, and commuted to school. To their credit, my parents tried hard to understand my apparent rebellion. They believed in me and that knowledge permitted me the freedom to seek my genuine life.

Of course, I was certainly not alone in my generation. Our rebellion propelled the world into a new era. Peace marches, sexual freedom, struggles against the establishment, and loud rock music came to represent my generation.

My rebellion literally "found a voice" when I began singing along with the Rolling Stones. Of course, the door of my bedroom was closed, but the very walls couldn't contain the force that rock music unleashed within me.

Georgetown and my first band

I was fascinated with Georgetown, the DC equivalent of Greenwich Village. Georgetown was the actual epicenter of the sixties cultural revolution. Seven days a week, young people with very long hair, wearing bell bottoms, love beads, girls in micro skirts and guys in wild flowered shirts, crowded the sidewalks. Everyone seemed to be smiling. Everyone seemed to be in love. There were photographers everywhere. There may never be such a positive and happy time again in my lifetime. My generation was baptized by the availability of pot. I immersed myself in the qualities of the sixties, eschewing the drugs, but fully embracing the concept of universal love.

And so, I had truly come into a new persona. I always spent my weekends in the Georgetown music clubs or just walking around the picturesque streets of Georgetown. The music drew me like a moth to a flame. From Monday to Friday afternoon, I attended the University of Maryland and practiced my singing with the Rolling Stones. Weekends I spent in Georgetown, desperately trying to look the part.

And so, it was to begin one sunny Saturday afternoon, when the early high school-aged son of one of our neighbors invited me over to meet his new band. The existing group consisted of my neighbor playing guitar, and two brothers, who played guitar and drums. They had been practicing in my neighbor's basement for a month but they were one element short of a rock 'n roll band – *a singer*. My neighbor's name was Eddie and the entire neighborhood was ablaze with the news of my "hippie" transformation. Eddie saw in me the opportunity to supply what the band needed: A singer who really looked the part – me.

I sat in on one of their practices and sang a few of the Rolling Stones songs I had been singing along with in my room for months. Eddie and the boys were ecstatic. They suddenly had a singer.

We practiced every weekend in Eddie's parents garage. To the neighbors, it sounded loud. I wonder what they thought when, years later, my bands practiced at my parents' house just two blocks away from Eddie's and played at concert volume, causing dust to sprinkle down from the basement ceiling and neighbor kids from blocks around would come to peer in the basement windows.

Every rocker will have fond stories of finding appropriate practice facilities. I once sang with a short-lived band where we had no proper facilities and had to practice in an apartment bedroom. The guitarists would play without amplification, the drummer would pound away on a mattress and we would sing without any electronic aid.

And speaking of pounding away, that's exactly what the neighbors would do to the walls when we practiced.

That band was doomed before it started.

The very first gig...

We had been practicing for about a month when Eddie announced that he had somehow arranged a gig in a popular department store girls' clothing department. The company had decided to use the popularity of music to pull in customers. The four of us in the band were breathless. The gig paid no money, but the exposure would surely further our "career".

So, the arrangement was made and the boys and I headed to Georgetown to buy appropriate clothing. We practiced our ten songs over and over. Without a PA system, I sang through one channel of Eddie's guitar amplifier.

Suddenly the day was upon us – our first real gig! (No money, but "great publicity").

We dressed up in our finest new bell bottom pants and wild flowered shirts. In addition, I wore a pair of "Beatle boots". We were more than excited.

Years later, I would share the story with other musicians, and discovered that virtually each one had experienced similar "first gig" stories. Their stories and mine, went something like this:

That Saturday morning, we loaded our two amps and set of drums into two cars and headed out. I was so excited, I sang all the way to the store to relieve the tension and loosen up my voice. We pulled up to the store loading platform and Eddie ran off to find the store manager. Forty minutes later we were set up on a small improvised "stage" in the Girls Department. To his credit, the Girls Department manager was pretty cool, despite his shock at seeing my fourteen-inch long black hair and my wild outfit.

We quickly tuned up and started playing. I only remember one song we did that afternoon. It was my favorite, "Satisfaction" by the Rolling Stones. I did my best Mick Jagger moves. But suddenly the manager of the Ladies Department came running up, demanding that we lower the volume, as we were chasing away his customers. By this time, we had drawn a small crowd of teenaged girls and everyone was very disappointed when we had to stop.

Volume would become the pivotal issue that would raise its ugly head time and time again when playing in enclosed spaces. Years later, in a tiny bar in Bethany Beach, Delaware, my band very nearly broke up when assaulted by management wanting music, but not "loud" music. On that occasion, we eventually were reduced to playing thru amplifiers with covers over the speakers, our drummer had to gently tap his drums, and I had to sing without a microphone! We had been promised that a "wild teenage crowd" would pour in for the Saturday jam session and we could play in our normal manner.

We lived for Saturday and tried to ignore the "fifty-and-over" (way over!) crowd of bar patrons. These are the times that test rock musicians and guarantee acceptance in "Rock 'n Roll Heaven".

Georgetown and girls!

Before and after the episode of "The Arrangement" (the band with Eddie et al.) I was spending every weekend in Georgetown soaking up the ambiance and the rock music. My most sincere ambition was to be a rock singer and my opportunities would soon come about. During this phase I was with a new girl almost every weekend. Usually I would meet them at The Cave or at another club. Often, I would drive us to a special place I had discovered. It was high atop the hill that defines the border of Georgetown. There, along "P" Street and under the ancient oaks, was my favorite parking spot. It was right in front of the "Home for the Blind". I loved this spot because no one could spy on us while we made out in my car.

As my hair got longer, I found that I was more attractive to the beautiful, long-haired, blue-eyed "counter culture" girls of Georgetown. It was a thoroughly magical time in my life. And it only got better when I discovered the music.

One of my favorite music "haunts" was a small, scruffy, establishment located on "M" Street, in the very heart of Georgetown. "The Cave" was a club fashioned out of a small, ancient two-story building. There was a small stage built into the space where a front window once reached out to the M Street sidewalk. There was also a smaller stage in the grungy basement. Two bands would alternate sets, providing nearly continuous music until 2 AM.

Some of the best local bands of the time played in "The Cave" and that's where I was to be found every Friday night. Saturday nights, I would move down to "The Bayou". The Bayou was located on K Street, across the street from the Potomac River. The Bayou had had a questionable history including a long phase as the home of DC's stripper entertainers. It was where business men and Congressional types would meet to ogle the entertainment. One of the favorite legends of The Bayou was the story of a southern congressman who fell for one of the strippers and famously drove his Cadillac off a bridge and into the Potomac in a drunken episode.

That incident occurred years before I took up residence at The Bayou.

"The Cherry People"

By the time I was a junior in college, I switched my allegiance to a club on M Street, called "The Silver Dollar". I and many other members of my generation, were drawn by a local band called "The Cherry People". To my taste, my friends The Cherry People, were the best band around. Years later, after they had broken up, the lead guitarist, Punky Meadows, was recruited by an international band with recording and touring contracts. Punky went on to be a world-famous guitarist with a band called Angel. Punky's face was so perfect, that a stylized version of his face became Angel's record cover and insignia.

It's hard to estimate the impact on local rock music of The Cherry People. They were clearly "The Georgetown band". If you could interview all the local musicians of the sixties, you would find that virtually all of them were influenced by The Cherry People. They played for years at The Silver Dollar nightclub and every night other local musicians were there soaking up the vibe.

Eventually I became good friends with the band's lead singer, Doug. I learned a lot from Doug and enjoyed his friendship. Years before, The Cherry People had had a number one song, "And Suddenly". Ironically, the song was not representative of the blasting rock music that The

Cherry People churned out. But they had toured the country in support of their record. That distinction raised them far above the other bands in Georgetown.

When Doug learned that I was a singer, he took me under his wing, although I was a decade older than him in age, but assuredly not in experience. I knew all their songs and would often sing along, which wasn't weird because the volume of the band meant that no one else would ever hear me. By the time I was established as a singer, Doug would sometimes slip out to get home before the 2 AM closing time. On those nights, he called me up to sing with the band in his place. What a thrill! Compared to the bands I had been working with, singing with The Cherry People was like suddenly driving a racing car after riding a bike.

But the day would come when I had my own "racing car" band.

And so it began…

After watching others perform, spending untold hours singing along with Mick Jagger and constantly being asked if I was a musician, I decided the time had come.

My first paid performances were at The Cave. It sat on M Street, right in the middle of the "M Street Strip". That was a block of Georgetown's M Street which featured four nightclubs with nightly music until 2 AM. The Cave couldn't have been much more minimalist. It featured a dark street-level room painted black and featuring psychedelic, day-glo paints and "black lights" that were plugged into the old ceiling fixtures. The paints glowed in bright, psychedelic colors. It was a "teenage" nightclub – no alcohol (except what was smuggled in by the teen patrons.) The bands alternated sets for continuous music. It was loud and crowded!

I was asked to audition for a band that played the "basement" at The Cave. For some unknown reason, the band thought I had experience, I certainly looked the part and I was thrilled! My audition was singing three currently popular rock songs. Apparently, I made an impact. We only practiced once before we began playing the "basement" gig at The Cave.

We played forty minutes per hour from 8 PM until 2 AM plus a "jam session" on Saturday afternoon. We had to repeat songs since we hadn't had rehearsal time. Playing seven hours a night, I discovered that I was unable to speak during the day in order to save my voice for nighttime. I don't remember what we were paid, but it wasn't much.

I can't remember the name of that band, but I know it didn't last very long.

In the meantime, I auditioned for a group call "Zog's House". The group included a young man who would come to be one of my best friends. His name was Dennis and he was the equipment manager for The Cherry People – that's how we met. Dennis had dark hair about the length of mine and played bass. He had seen me filling in for Doug and thought we might put a band together. Dennis knew a guitarist, who knew another guitarist, who knew a drummer. And before long we had the makings of a band. We rehearsed at Todd's house in Virginia. Todd was from a well-to-do family and owned a really nice guitar and a Vox Super Beatle.

What's that? You may be asking. When the Beatles prepared to come to America and begin playing large arenas and stadiums, they needed power in the form of an amplifier and speakers that could rattle your fillings from one hundred yards. That's when the Vox Super Beatle was born. Just having a Super

Beatle conferred a high level of panache to a band. Incredibly, it was the amplifier of choice for many concert bands and aspiring concert bands for many years before it was supplanted by Marshall Amplifiers. The wattage coming out of a Marshall can *knock you down* from one hundred yards. Marshall and the well-named Hi Watt amplifiers, made famous by The Who, continue to be among the amplifiers of choice.

I was excited to be the singer for Zog's House. We all got along well and our musical tastes were similar, a problem which dooms many bands and precipitates the constant changing of band members.

My parents had been kind enough to loan me the money to buy a PA system. Every month I would make my payments at the famous "Chuck Levin's Music City". It was, and to a large extent, still is, THE place to buy musical equipment.

Dennis shared an old apartment with a "band manager" who immediately wanted to represent us. The agent's name was Bruce. The problem was that Bruce didn't have any reliable connections in the music business. He booked us for several auditions but we made no money out of his efforts. I remember one audition that was on a wintery day in an unheated barn! We were literally shivering and I feared that my wonderful PA system might be damaged by the cold.

Dennis agreed and we soon cut Bruce loose.

Zog's House played on television once!

We were approached by a booking agent who needed a rockin' band to play on TV. The gig was an afternoon show for teens. It featured local bands playing live on an independent television station. Of course, we were delighted by the prospect, but also of course, it was an unpaid gig. The band reasoned that if we rocked the house, we would get tons of referral gigs. And so, we set about searching for just the right song.

Coincidentally, the band Steppenwolf had just released their first album, which featured a song called "Born to be Wild". The song was heaven-sent. It featured the same instruments we had in Zog's House and I was able to sing it. Born to be Wild became an anthem for an entire generation and we were the first ones to play it on television!

We practiced fiendishly. Four hours a day, playing Born to be Wild. I began to hear it in my sleep.

Finally, the day came and we excitedly packed the truck and headed off to play on television. We were incredibly lucky to have a truck from Todd's father's fruit and vegetable business to use. Not only that, Todd's older brother worked as our equipment man.

Each of us had bought a cool new outfit for the event. Todd, who is classically thin and handsome, wore a new fringed leather vest. My bass-playing friend Dennis wore a black leather outfit. Our drummer, Rod, wore a leather shirt, and our lead guitarist, Michael, wore leather pants and a collarless blue shirt with puffy sleeves. I capped off the visual impact by wearing just a leather vest, no shirt, and tight black silk pants.

After that show, the girls really started to notice us.

Our practice paid off and no unfortunate incidents marred our performance. The station replayed our segment for years. Somewhere out there, there's still a tape of that magical afternoon.

Several gigs came our way as a result of our TV appearance and of course we always played "Born to be Wild", but eventually the band broke up. But at least we all had something special to remember from our days in Zog's House...

Dennis and I continued to be good friends. A few years later, Dennis was working as the DJ in one of the clubs along M Street. He would make sure I got in free and had all the cokes I could drink.

My love of Georgetown continues to this day. How many nights did I spend caught up in the excitement of rock 'n roll as played by The Cherry People and all the other bands in Georgetown? It's impossible to say, but those days and nights made a huge impact on my life.

That affection for live rock music has never left me. In the future I would see acts as famous as The Jimmy Hendricks Experience, Sly and the Family Stone, The Who, Led Zeppelin, Bruce Springsteen and many more. But my desire was always to be up on that stage…

Losing my voice tainted my experiences of nightclub gigs. Years later, I would be in a band that played eight forty-minute sets per night and I sang almost all the songs. I couldn't speak during the day, but around seven PM, I would gradually be able to make semi-intelligible musical sounds.

The Be-Ins, gatherings of the tribes...

The '60s introduced the "Be-Ins". Spontaneous gatherings of youth featuring free-form dancing, wild clothes, the longest of long hair, marijuana, and beautiful people of both sexes. Zog's House was fortunate enough to play several of the Washington Be-Ins, which were held in a small park near Georgetown and next to Rock Creek. It is known as the P Street Beach. It's difficult to capture in words the way we all felt in those crazy, exciting days of the '60's. We thought everything was possible, the sun was always shining, and the world was fresh and new.

Sadly, Zog's House didn't last much longer than our appearances at the "Be-Ins". Nevertheless, we met many lovely young ladies at those shows. At the time my stage outfit featured red, white and blue striped bell bottom pants and a "puffy-sleeved" shirt reminiscent of Mick Jagger's outfit on one of the Ed Sullivan appearances. I would whip my very long black hair as I raced around the stage. I still have pictures taken during those shows and my face is always obscured by my hair.

It was not unusual for a beautiful long-haired girl to come up after the gig and ask for an autograph. I couldn't understand it, but it certainly was a delight. The girls of the '60s just always seemed to smile. They will probably never know how I, and certainly many of my bandmates, relied on those wonderful smiles.

During those special days of the '60s, I had many girlfriends. The girls of the '60s just seemed to be extra friendly and those microskirts just blew me away!

Many a memorable gig finished in the front seat of my car. I was always curious about the girls who, like me, came to Georgetown every weekend. I felt we were members of some social movement much larger than ourselves. That belief was echoed by the press who described us as a unique cultural phenomenon. How often a beautiful romantic scenario was spoiled by me asking a girl about her cultural beliefs!

Some girls really wanted to talk about the Vietnam War and my attitude to it. Well, I was a conscientious objector for deeply spiritual reasons.

Meanwhile, the spectacular finale to the "Zog's House" era occurred on the very same night that The Who were playing their only DC appearance of the year. It was a cool, cloudy Fall day, but it was about to heat up quickly for us.

As usually happens for bands, we had changed lead guitarists. We now had a talented guitarist named Howard.

Howard's father hated the band and wouldn't let his son out to practice. Consequently, I used to drive around to the street behind Howard's house. Howard would come running out with his guitar, jump in my car and away we would go.

Howard was Jewish and the time came around to have his bar mitzva. Howard father really wanted to play it big, so he rented a community center. To please his father, Howard arranged, although reluctantly, for the band to play at the ceremony. The big hitch was that his father's plan required the band to play after dark because his father had a black light show he wanted to present using the band. The really big hitch was that we weren't informed in advance and Howard's special day was the same night as the Who concert, which we had all planned to attend.

When we arrived at the community center, Howard's father had taped black cloth over the windows to darken the interior. I commented to my friend Dennis, our bass player.

"Something bad's gonna come of this."

The ceremony started with all Howard's father's friends and relatives in attendance. A group of about fifty people, many over seventy years old. The band sat over on the side and kept looking at our watches. The hour got later and later, as the ceremony wore on. Eventually we had waited as long as we could.

"Howard" I hissed. "We've gotta get outta here to get to the Who concert."

"I know man. My father's doing what he always does. He always screws me up. Plus he's been drinking. I'll go tell him…"

"Ok, man. Be careful. He really looks wound up."

Howard crept over to his father who was whipping up the crowd of friends and relatives.

"Dad. My friends have to go soon. Wrap it up and let us play."

His father stopped talking and turned to Howard, raising his arm in warning.

"I'm your father. This is your family. No one moves until I tell them they can move, understand Howard?"

He was obviously furious with his son and the band.

He finished with "Now go sit down!"

Howard returned to where the band was anxiously waiting.

"He won't listen guys. He's had too much to drink and it's gotta be his way or no way. I think the best thing to do is take down the equipment and load it back into the truck."

"Sorry Howard." Todd answered, unplugging his amp and lifting it off the speaker stack. The other band members started doing the same. When Bill, the equipment manager began carrying out amplifiers and speaker cabinets, Howard's father came rushing over.

"Stop! Stop goddamn it! Nobody moves until I say so!"

Bill ignored the warning and continued carrying equipment out to the truck.

Howard's father flew into a screaming match with his son while each band member grabbed his equipment and bolted for the door.

Howard and his father continued screaming at each other until Howard began taking his amplifier off its speaker cabinet.

Howard's father went into action. He grabbed the amplifier and they began struggling over the amplifier power module. Eventually Howard and his father swung around and around, screaming at each other as the band stood watching, frozen, fearing the possible destruction of Howard's expensive amp.

"Go on guys! Get out before he turns on you!" Howard shouted to us. "Go now. I think I'm out of the band!"

The other band members ran past the horrified family and out to their cars, shouting "Sorry Howard. Good luck!"

We dashed away, Bill with the truck headed home, and the rest of us headed for the Who concert.

Our last sight of Howard was the nightmare vision of he and his father struggling, shouting, and exchanging curses while swinging his amplifier around, just one slip from an equipment disaster.

We didn't find out what happened for a week.

"Jim" he said when I answered my phone. "It's Howard."

"Howard…the last time I saw you I was terrified. How are you?"

"Not good, Jim. I'm afraid I'm out of the band."

"Oh God, Howard. We were just starting to do so well!"

"I know, man. My father's impossible. He's literally mental. I'm gonna run away and take my guitar and hitchhike west. Wish me luck."

"Oh, Howard. I'm gonna miss you, brother."

"Thanks, Jim. Good luck to the band."

"Goodbye Howard…"

The Who concert was awesome, nevertheless that was one of the worst days in my musical career.

That Sunday took all the steam out of the band. We broke up a month later. My friend Dennis and I went to join a group called "Ransom". Sadly, most bands break apart for one reason or another. Of those who are able to weather the storms, it's still a tiny fraction that have any financial or creative success.

That's what makes rock 'n roll alternately compelling and heartbreaking.

Joe the Drummer

After Zog's House played its last gig, I got the chance to play with a couple of semi-well known local musicians. Jim was the guitarist, Paul "The Kid" was the bass player, and we had Tom Lepson on keyboards. In later years, Tom would go on to play major venues and became a hero of DC rock music. And then there was Joe. I've never since had as much fun on stage as Joe provided.

Joe had a beard and long hair and was a vegan. One Christmas he worked as Santa for a major Virginia shopping center. For the Santa gig, Joe had to add lots of padding since he was actually quite slim. The story goes that each day he hitchhiked to work wearing his Santa suit. One day some Virginia ruffians squirted shaving cream all over his head – Joe had to go back home and get cleaned up before he could appear before the children. He was very eccentric and very intelligent. He used to decorate his drumkit with leafy tree branches. When we played, he peered out from behind his drum jungle, making hilarious comments and noises which never failed to crack me up. Often it was hard to sing, and not just laugh, when Joe was in his glory.

We were booked to open a new nightclub on M Street in Georgetown. The audience was appreciative and we worked that gig for two months before Tom left to pursue a solo career. We all wished him well, but it meant the end of the band. It was no surprise considering that most bands eventually break up.

During 1972, as the band with Joe began its descent into oblivion, a middle-aged man came to me with a peculiar offer. He was obsessed with the idea that the song "Running Bear" which had been a hit in the early '60's, could be revived and take advantage of the role native peoples were playing in the concept of a New Age. The promoter had sunk his own money into the project and was very anxious to have me as the Native American image to help launch the song.

I was thrilled. The gig not only guaranteed me recording studio time, but also an appearance on local TV! The fact that I have some Native American heritage synched the deal. So, one Fall weekend, I spent a full day in a recording studio singing along to the music track that Mike, the promoter, had already gotten recorded by studio musicians. Mike and Joe the Drummer got along famously. Mike was constantly cracking up with Joe's jokes.

To promote the record, Mike arranged a TV appearance featuring me in "native" dress, lip synching while the record played on the music track. I was ecstatic – the chance to honor my heritage, as slim as it was, was an opportunity I wasn't going to pass up!

Finally, the night came and I dressed in my leather vest, no shirt, leather pants, moccasins and head band.

The taping went well and I was thrilled when the segment played on TV.

Alas, all the hard work and Mike's money was for naught. It seems a country music star had, curiously, decided to record the song. It was a big hit for him. Mike, quite rightly, felt he had been shafted, seeing that the county music singer's manager was the man to whom Mike had originally pitched the idea of "Running Bear".

Joe, sadly, just faded out of my life. I'll never forget him.

It seems that musicians are a nomadic breed, always moving on, looking for the next big thing and seldom finding it.

After the band with Joe broke up, I was without a group for a year. Basically, I just spent my weekends watching The Cherry People play and wishing I had a band as special as Doug, Chris, Rocky, Jan and Punky. Doug was kind enough to let me sit in for him occasionally, which made my exile more bearable.

I also spent much of my time in and around Georgetown. I took a job at a music store on M Street. My job was only to prevent theft. Thieves would bring raincoats into the store and lay them over the record bins. Then, as they picked up their coats they would grab multiple albums and wrap them up into the coats then run out of the store.

While I worked at the record store, a number of young women frequented the store trying to catch my eye. I remember one attractive brunette who came in the store several times, then one evening she whispered several sexual activities she wanted to perform with me. Of course, not knowing her, I demurred. An hour later, her husband came into the store looking for her.

Another time a lovely young "counter-culture girl" came into the store, hung around for about an hour, then asked me to take her home. I, of course, replied no.

The manager of the store was an intelligent but degenerate fellow. Every Saturday he would regale me with his sexual adventures from the previous week, not that I was interested.

It seemed to me that the record store was action central for weird and perverted citizens of Georgetown. Of course, the years I worked there were blossoming years of the sexual revolution.

Perhaps the most amazing event in my time at the record store, was the month I was pursued by a stripper. She had seen me in the store and was fascinated by my beautiful way-past shoulder-length hair. She always stood too close and loved to caress my rear end. Somehow, she got my phone number (I think from the store manager) and began calling me at home. After the fifth time she called, I told her that despite her attractive, if too openly sexual, demeanor I wasn't interested. After that, she stopped calling.

A few years later, I hooked up with a woman at a nightclub. Leila invited me to her apartment but told me that we had to be quiet because her young daughter was sleeping with her mother in the next room. We made love passionately while I kept one eye on the bedroom door.

What followed with Leila was my most foolish escapade. She being a fan of my friends The Cherry People, always stayed at the Silver Dollar club until it closed at two AM. I was living with my parents at the time. One Saturday, I had stayed home for some reason and my phone rang at two ten AM. It was Leila saying she really wanted to see me. I knew what that meant, but I explained that I wasn't going out at two AM.

"Well why don't I come to you?" She purred.

"My God, Leila. I live with my parents and they are asleep upstairs!"

The negotiations continued for a few minutes while I recalled our passionate couplings. Finally, I was morally weak and relented.

She arrived about twenty-five minutes later and parked right in front of my parents' house, then walked up to the door. I had been watching for her and quickly and quietly opened the door lest she ring the bell.

What occurred next was amazingly foolish on my part. With both my parents just one floor away, I removed her clothes and she removed mine.

"We must be very quiet" I whispered.

She gave me that smile and a look that said "You let me come to your house, now let's enjoy it."

In retrospect, I was incredibly trusting. Fortunately, the family sofa was solid and didn't squeak with our passionate lovemaking.

By three fifteen, she was gone and I was left considering my folly.

Only weeks later, I would spend most of a cold winter's night parked outside her apartment, waiting for her to return home on a Saturday night. I was pretty certain she was seeing someone else and I wanted to catch them as they arrived at her home. At four AM, I finally gave up my vigil and groggily drove home. Despite not having solid evidence, I terminated our relationship.

Two summers later, I met a beautiful art student. Zog's House had played at the nightclub in her town and she had seen me there. When we met again in Georgetown, she boldly addressed me saying.

"Heh! I saw your band in Lexington Park. You were way cool!"

I thanked her and asked her name.

"I'm Candy. Your name's Jim, right?"

"Yes" I responded fascinated by her green eyes and long brown hair.

"Would you like to get coffee?" I asked.

"Would love to, but I've got to get back to a class at art school."

"Where do you study?"

"The Corcoran School of Art. I'm a sophomore."

"How cool!" I responded. We always said that in the '60s.

"Here's my phone number. Call me some time." She called back as she hurried away.

"Yes. I certainly will." I thought.

Three weeks later, we were dating.

It happened that my parents had planned a summer trip to Pennsylvania to see relatives. I invited Candy to visit me at my parents' house while they were out of town. She readily accepted and one thing led to another and she was still there when they arrived home from their trip.

I tried to play it cool, telling them that Candy had just come over to see me that day. Of course, that was a lie. We had been in bed almost continuously since she arrived three days before my parents. Candy packed up, kissed me goodbye and told me to call.

By fall, we had been passionately dating for some time.

Candy was transferring from the Corcoran Art School to a famous art school that was part of the University of Pennsylvania. She would be living in a dormitory but wanted me to visit.

Thus, followed sixth months of commuting to Philadelphia every weekend. At the time I was between bands and was a junior at the University of Maryland. I also worked part time in DC, loading trucks at a warehouse.

So, the minute the Friday workday ended, I would dash out to my car and point it toward Philadelphia. In those days there was no super highway to Philadelphia, so I drove the old Route 1 trip. I came to know every dangerous turn on that old road.

When I arrived and had parked my car a reasonable distance from the campus. I would grab my pack and run toward her all-female dorm. I would call her from the lobby and she would smuggle me into her dorm room, where I would spend the weekend. She would bring me food from the cafeteria. Her dormmates realized what was happening but played it cool.

Now it happens that Candy's brother was a junkie. He had started with pills but quickly graduated to heroin. He also worked as a merchant marine where he would stay high during most of the voyages. Candy had tried to convince him to get clean, but he was never able to sustain it. I was appalled by the situation and was fearful of his influence over Candy. Unfortunately, I was never able to break their bond and it gradually destroyed our affair.

Irony is such a peculiar thing…

A number of years later, Candy married one of my old bandmates. I never discovered how they met, but I wished them well. Ironically, his name was Randy.

Meanwhile, after Candy, I returned to rock 'n roll.

Blues, acid and women...

In the spring of 1976, I joined a blues band.

It was three blues fanatics, me, and the leader of the group was a white guy who had once played guitar for a well-known soul band.

An odd combination? You betcha!

The blues guys just wanted to play songs from Lead Belly, The Soul Survivors and Cyrus Chitlin, among others. The guitarist wanted to mix in a few James Brown songs which I was expected to sing and a Janice Joplin song which he was expecting to sing. I wanted to play Rolling Stones and Mitch Ryder and the Detroit Wheels.

To say our material was eclectic was an understatement!

One day we came to practice only to find that the bass player wouldn't be making practice because he'd been up all night on acid and had tried to climb a building.

We played an occasional gig, but nothing steady, mostly college frat parties at the University of Maryland.

And then there was *the acid gig*. It was a college gig arranged by the white guy. We practiced a couple songs before we packed up the van and

40

headed to the gig. At the end of practice, it appears, the white guy, who was the band leader, decided to take a hit of acid. He had broken a string at the end of practice and planned to replace it once we were at the gig.

I immediately knew something was amiss when I arrived at the frat house. The white guy (let's call him Russell) was standing in the middle of the floor with his guitar in his hand and his mind somewhere out past Jupiter! While we set up the equipment, Russell just stood there. Finally, one of the "blues guys" walked him over to the stage and helped him finish stringing his guitar.

I was pretty sure things weren't going to go well. Russell finally was coaxed up onto the stage where he stood rooted like a toadstool. It was time to start playing and we had to call Russell by transmartian radiophone. He was there but he wasn't there…

"Listen" I hissed at Russell. "You've got to pull it together, man!"

"Ok…" Was all he said.

We all waited for him to count down to the start of the first song, a blues shuffle useful to loosen up the fingers and get everyone on the same track. The band had played most of the first twelve bars, when suddenly, Russell shifted into a completely different song! Everyone in the band (except Russell) just looked at each other and tried to play along. This

same phenomenon occurred for the first ten songs.
Russell shifted songs, shifted keys, shifted
tempos…it was quite phenomenal. But the thing
that blew me away, was the fact that at the end of
the first set, the crowd gave us a rousing hand.

"Are these people in the same room I'm in?" I
asked one of the blues guys.

"Yeah, that set was pretty trippy. I guess the crowd
thinks it's some kind of new music mix – you know
cutting from one song to another randomly."

God knows how we got thru that night, but I
decided that I'd never put myself into a situation
that embarrassing again. I quit the band the next
day.

Marriage, rock, tennis and hair

When the '80s rolled around, I was married to a sweet young woman named Karen. We had met when we were both students at the University of Maryland. Karen was into rock and into me. What could be better. She was lovely and had wonderful eyes and a wonderful laugh. No brothers to cause problems, for she was an only child. The ironic hitch was that Karen's father was an officer in the District of Columbia Police Force. Even more ironic, was the fact that the beat he was responsible for included the Georgetown district where I had always hung out. Karen enjoyed the Georgetown clubs but her father was always sending cops into the clubs to pull her out.

When we met we were both juniors at The University of Maryland. I spent many nights in her apartment. I would have to leave any time her roommate's father would come over. Their apartment was on the second floor and one evening the father showed up unexpectedly. I couldn't get out of the apartment except by climbing out the window! It was Fall and I reluctantly climbed out and clung to the cold window sill for an hour, until the father left. Eventually my fingers thawed out.

Finally, Karen gave me an ultimatum: get married or breakup. Late in my twenties, I decided it was time to take the plunge. I loved Karen and I figured we would make out all right.

So, we got married on a lovely Fall day at the chapel at the University of Maryland. Karen's parents were kind enough to give us a down payment on a house, so we bought a Gaithersburg, Maryland townhouse.

The evening after the wedding ceremony, we had agreed to drive to Florida for our honeymoon. I guess the hustle and bustle of preparing for the wedding affected my mind – why else would I agree to drive all night after such a stressful day?

We set off around four PM. Fortunately the weather was good, unfortunately I don't remember much about that night. Karen fell asleep before North Carolina and I was left alone to battle the demons of sleep deprivation. All I remember was huge trucks roaring past our Toyota. Sometime after five AM, I vaguely remember pulling into a motel parking lot in Lake Buena Vista, Florida. At last I could sleep!

It's peculiar how the length of your hair was so important during the '60s and right thru until the end of the '80s. I wore my hair exceptionally long, as did my musician friends. However, we paid a price, socially, for our non-conformity. Most places we went, we were plagued by disapproving looks and comments. Occasionally, we were threatened. I always wondered if The Beatles, who popularized longer hair, were ostracized as we were.

Despite the length of my hair, I was hired working an office job in Bethesda, Maryland. I was a proofreader for one of the first electronic publishing companies in the Washington area.

And then it happened: the vice president of the company asked me to play tennis at lunch time. I went along, not knowing what I was doing. And so, began what would become a passion for the game of tennis. With my baseball skills, I picked up tennis quickly. Before I'd been playing one year, I began to play on a team. It wasn't long before I entered tennis tournaments. I couldn't live without tennis. For the period of two years, I played every single day, including shoveling snow off a court in order to play.

Before you think I was alone in my tennis mania, I must mention my good friend Perry. Perry and I met at a local tennis tournament when I had been playing about a year. He was already a solid competitor in the local tournaments. We got to talking and I explained that I needed a practice partner who wanted to play as often as possible. He felt the same way and was willing to put up with my inexperience.

That began a close friendship that lasted for many years. Once I had developed skills at the game, Perry and I played constantly.

A couple years later, Perry accepted a position as a club pro. We still practiced together whenever he was available.

Years after he retired from teaching, he and I literally practiced together every day for two years. When it rained, we would sweep off the court and practice. When it snowed, we shoveled the court and practiced. Without Perry's influence, I would never have developed my tennis skills. We also became close friends. He helped me move several times. You know that's a good friend.

After Karen and I were married, I took a job working for a Federal agency, the Department of Commerce. I worked quite close to where Karen and I had bought our first house and it was only a five-minute commute. While working for NIST I met Tom Lipe. Tom and I were part of a group of tennis players who met every day at lunch time to play tennis. They still do.

Tom and I became close friends and tennis partners. Eventually, we would enter tournaments together. We also played as a doubles team for the NIST tennis team in the Federal League.

The story of Dee

During our tenure at The Golden Eagle, I was very careful about any entanglements with female customers. But after we had been playing there for about six months, I met a customer named Dee. Dee and one of her girlfriends came in one Saturday night. They sat over in the corner away from the gang customers. She wore glasses with big black frames. Most girls with glasses ignored me for some reason and the feeling was mutual. Dee and her friend were only asked to dance about twice that night, but when Dee came out on the dance floor, she gave me a big smile. I noticed that she was quite attractive regardless of the glasses. Later, during a break, I went over to her table and introduced myself and thanked them for coming and making my evening more pleasant. Dee kind of giggled at that remark.

I didn't think much about the incident until Dee showed up again the next weekend, alone. I noticed that she was there and dressed in a fairly provocative pantsuit which looked very nice on her. I went over to her table during a break. I asked her about her employment and we exchanged pleasant conversation until it was time to play again.

"We'll do a song just for you, Dee." I said as I took my leave.

She smiled and blushed.

We played "Heartbreaker" by the Rolling Stones and I announced that the song was for Dee.

On the next break, I went over to her table. When I sat down, she put her hand on top of mine and said.

"Thank you so much for the song but who is the heartbreaker, you or me?"

I nearly fell out of my chair.

"I guess we'll have to wait and see." I replied, with a wink.

She smiled and blushed.

As I've recounted before in this narrative, we played until four AM on weekends. Dee came over to the band's table after the two AM set. She smiled a bashful smile and handed me a note.

"Goodnight" She said and smiled as she turned to leave.

Of course, my bandmates immediately began kidding me.

"Jim's got a girl!"

"Hey Jim, why didn't you take her home?"

"Way to go, Jim!"

"Calm down you guys." I responded. "She just needs a friend."

They all laughed and we started playing one of the two "mellow music" sets designed to give the "breakfast" patrons a chance to get their food and eat their two AM "breakfasts" which was what The Golden Eagle was known for.

When I opened Dee's note it had her phone number and the phrase "please call me".

Later, driving home, I wondered what Dee was all about. I had the feeling that she was alone and just wanted a friend.

A few days later, when my voice had recovered from the punishment of eight sets of music, I phoned Dee. I didn't get an answer so I left a message.

"Dee, it's Jim from The Golden Eagle. I got your note so I thought I'd give you a call. Call me back at 301.555-2787. Hoping you're having a great day."

She called back that evening around seven. We had a nice conversation, during which she explained that she was an orphan and had recently moved into an apartment in Alexandria, Virginia. She told me about her job and how she was alone a lot.

I, of course, realized that her story was similar to many like stories I had heard from other girls interested in dating band members.

But she conveyed a genuine touch of sadness that made me feel her sorrow.

We talked about my passion for rock and about the bands I had been with. She giggled a very lovely giggle when I made jokes about my humorous previous band experiences.

Finally, I decided I liked Dee. She had obviously had a difficult life but she didn't complain. I decided to ask her out. She was genuinely delighted.

With our schedule at the club, we only had Mondays off, so I asked Dee if she would like to see a movie the next Monday.

Her reply was muffled, but I was sure I heard a sob.

"Dee, are you ok?"

"Oh, yes Jim. Very ok. Yes, I'd love to see a movie."

The next Monday evening, I was driving to Alexandria to take Dee to a movie.

It was a Peter Sellers comedy, one of my favorites. We laughed our way thru the entire movie. That left the goodnight kiss. But I had already decided to take it slow with Dee. I definitely didn't want to add to her sorrows, so I kissed her goodnight and took my leave. She made it clear that she would have liked me to stay, but I wasn't up for a quickie and a "goodnight", so I left with a smile and a promise to call her again.

After that, we spoke nearly every day by phone. She would share with me her experiences working in a lawyer's office and I charmed her with my storehouse of "true rock stories".

I had long ago discovered that many young women were impressed by the life of a musician and not at all unhappy to be "a notch on a bedpost". I had had my share of one-nighters but there was, to me, something very sad in the constant go-round of sexual encounters.

Over time I discovered that Dee wanted to have something she could hold on to, and I was that something. It's not that our relationship was not passionate. Quite the opposite.

We dated for about six months. I'd like to think I gave her some pleasure that was missing from her life, and when she admitted to me that she wanted to move on, I only wished her the best. I knew that she had come to realize that she was not only attractive, but also worthy of having a lasting relationship.

I hope she's out there somewhere in a loving, kind relationship.

She deserves it.

New Year's Eve at the Golden Eagle

As you already know, one of my bands played for an extended period at the Golden Eagle Restaurant and Bar, which featured a nightly buffet and "breakfast" until 4 AM on the weekends. The manager, who was more interested in making money than getting home at a reasonable hour, firmly believed that if the Golden Eagle was open after 2 AM, people from all the other clubs, would flock to the restaurant for "breakfast".

That band was Tom on guitar, another Tom on drums, Mike on bass and me singing. I knew from the moment I first met Tom the guitarist that he was an outstanding talent. He not only carried all the guitar parts but also shared the vocals with me and we were to become close friends.

That schedule meant that the band would have to play eight sets per night. Since Tom and I shared all the vocal duties for the band, that meant that we would have to sing for eight forty-five-minute sets each night. Despite the fact that my voice had gotten much stronger, I was faced with the inability to talk during the day, in order to rest my vocal cords for the night's exertions.

The Golden Eagle was a strange gig. The restaurant occupied the street level floor of a building. The upper floors of the building were the offices of the

DC Narcotic Squad (the dreaded "narcs"). To offer their new narcotic agents some practice, they would send them to scout the Golden Eagle for narcotic users. After all, they assumed, where there was rock music, there would be drugs. Although I never partook of pot, I considered it a thoroughly benign drug and decided to do my part to "bust" the "narcs" circulating inside the nightclub section of the restaurant. The Narcotics Squad management dressed their agents to "fit in" with the audience they were scouting. Now, the fact is that everyone who was a regular at the club, knew that the guys with short hair and wearing flowered shirts and ill-fitting bell-bottoms were "narcs". We simply made jokes about it from the stage. The agents really, really wished that they could "bust" the band, but it wasn't going to happen.

The Golden Eagle was the "home turf" for a white gang from Prince George's County. Musicians learn early to "just play" and try to ignore the unsavory members of the audience. To our good fortune, the gang never made trouble during our tenure at the club. One problem did occur, however.

I inadvertently became the "object of affection" for one of the female members of the gang. She would follow me during breaks and try to get me to sit at her table. She asked me to take her home. She was a lovely girl, but I knew much better than to encourage her interest. I do remember that my hair was much longer than her bleached blond locks!

We had been playing at the "Eagle" for six months when the Christmas season arrived. The management offered the band a special deal for New Year's Eve. We would split the "door" with the club. We were excited with the prospect of receiving a bonus, especially considering the modest wages we were earning despite our very late-night efforts.

I splurged and bought a new all-black outfit with silk pants and shirt to go with my black Beatle boots.

New Year's Eve was to be the last night at "The Eagle" for at least a month. I was really looking forward to not having to conserve my voice all day as I had been doing.

This New Year's Eve would be a night to remember.

I pored over the weather forecast. As the week wore on, the weather possibilities began to deteriorate. By December 29th, the forecast was for snow. Surely, it would be light snow and not ruin the evening for us, surely...

Finally, New Year's Eve arrived with a weather report of heavy snow. As the late afternoon wore on, the sky became leaden and the clouds hung low and looked ominous. By 5 PM, it had started to snow heavily.

Our drummer Tom drove an old Volks bus that didn't always start. It was not unusual for me to have to run behind the Volks, pushing it until the engine kicked in.

Ultimately, the weather won out. By stage time, there was more than six inches of snow on every street in the downtown area.

We played, but the audience didn't arrive. It was a bust. Not even the gang members showed up. Not even my special admirer.

The restaurant's manager gave up and announced that the restaurant/club would close at eleven thirty.

We were crushed. Our holiday bonus was a washout. We packed up the equipment and prepared it to be picked up a few days later, when the streets were amenable.

Finally, we came to the moment when we would be leaving "The Eagle", possibly forever.

Just as we said goodbye to the management, Tom the drummer, tapped my shoulder.

"Uh, Jim. I need a jumpstart to get the Volks going."

I looked down at my brand new thin silk shirt and pants. "Ok. Let's go." I reluctantly replied.

I pulled on my coat and we exited the club into a blinding snow storm. The storm would eventually gain a place of infamy in the weather history of DC. Despite all that, we had to jumpstart the ancient Volks.

By the time we had reached the Volks, my hands and face were numb. Snow was covering my beautiful hair and my Beatle boots with the two-inch heels (specifically designed for dry weather). He climbed in and I took my position at the rear of the Volks and prepared to push it out onto a snow-choked 14th Street. To no surprise, the Volks didn't start with the first try.

He rolled down the driver's window and stuck his head out into the driving snow.

"Jim, you're gonna have to push it!" (The words I feared hearing.)

"Right!" I cried. "I'll push you out onto 14th Street!"

I began pushing the senior auto. My Beatle boots were filling with snow and my beautiful outfit was blowing in the storm. The Volks grumbled but didn't start. I tried to run faster but my boots were full of snow. Finally, after pushing for three blocks, the Volks finally turned over.

"Thanks, Jim. See ya!"

I struggled the half mile back to where my car was parked. By the time I arrived at my Toyota, I was shivering and soaked to the bone, one of my boots was gone. And the snow just kept belting down.

Fortunately, my Toyota started immediately and I slowly made my way thru the now-eight-inch deep accumulation. The roads were deserted, which was a plus for me. I turned the heater on full and tried to focus on just making it back to Bethesda.

I pulled into my driveway at 1:15 AM, soaked and still shivering.

The Golden Eagle gig was over.

666: The Band

Spring of 1991, I was searching for a band when fate blessed me by introducing me to a fabulous guitarist, Tom. Chris, who was a terrific bass player soon joined us. Now we were about to form the core of a band. All we really needed was a drummer, Tom being so talented that another instrument was not a necessity as it would be with almost any other band. Chris mentioned that one of his hometown friends was a hot drummer. When Chris brought Charlie to the first practice, I thought he was too young and way too scrawny to be much of a drummer. It only took one practice session to blow my mind – Charlie beat the hell out of his drums! To make matters even better, Charlie was a sweet-tempered guy, who just loved to play.

So now we had the nucleus of a new band. I was excited. We named the band "666" and we began practicing six days a week at Chris' parents home, which was far away in southern Maryland. It was quite a drive, but Tom and I made the trek every week. Chris' parents were very kind. They made us welcome in their home and all four of us slept on the floor of Chris' room. That arrangement made for some humorous evenings when Chris snored loudly and I woke up and began laughing. It wasn't long before all four of us were laughing. We practiced for three full days, then took one off, then practiced for three more days.

Once we had a song list, including great original songs that Tom had written, we began the often spirit-killing task of getting gigs. The lack of steady employment is the death blow to many, many bands. The difficulty of maintaining a repertoire of songs that would be familiar to a club audience steals the time away from writing and arranging original material, which was our focus.

To illustrate the problem of finding gigs, there's a famous and often-retold story of the band being booked by an agent who had never seen us play. He assumed that we were like the club bands he usually booked. At any rate, he booked us into a club in Rehoboth Beach, Delaware. The club was well-known for the "wild" weekend parties with large crowds of high school and college kids who were visiting the beach and wanted an exciting afternoon and night out, complete with an open bar and a rockin' band. That seemed like a good possibility for us, so we took the job.

When we arrived at "The Beach Club", we were shocked to discover that the first six nights of our week, we were expected to play to an audience of "fifty and over (some way over)". The situation was distinctly not our cup of tea. We very nearly turned around and went home, but in the end, decided to stick it out.

Our first night, we chose to play some classic rock 'n roll for the drinkers in the bar. Keep in mind that our equipment was concert-level wattage and no-holds-barred rock specific. Of course, we turned the amps down in deference to the few middle-aged folks who showed up to drink, as they obviously had all summer.

I believe we started with "Johnnie B. Goode", a classic from Chuck Berry. We had only played the first verse, when the red-faced club manager came up screaming, demanding that we turn down, way, way down. We looked at each other, I frowned, and we tried to accommodate the manager. Nevertheless, nothing worked and the manager just got madder and madder. When you tell a rock musician to turn down, it unleashes a built-in "fight or flight" response.

We took a break and went outside to talk over the situation. It was a tense scene. Half the group wanted to immediately pack up the equipment and go home. The other two of us emphasized the financial aspect of the gig. Eventually, we decided to stay, but in order to do that, the guitarists had to put covers over their amps, Charlie put a cover over his snare drum and Tom and I sang without using the PA system. It was a living hell for a rock band. Of course, the booking agent had neglected to inform us about the week-night situation. Knowing what type of band we were, he had only emphasized the weekend.

So, we decided to stay.

In retrospect, all I remember was that it was a very long week and the sleeping accommodations they supplied wasn't air conditioned. If your room doesn't have access to an ocean breeze, and there are four adult men sleeping on two beds, being at the beach rapidly loses its charm.

Of course, we met a few high school girls on the beach, but there were essentially no eligible women to meet during the course of the week, and the weekend crowd, although willing to rock hard, were mostly high school aged and college freshmen, too young for the attentions of the band.

It's that type of lesson that makes musicians play the blues, which we did a lot of at "The Beach Club".

Nevertheless, we cut loose on the weekend and rocked hard. After the kind of week we'd had, it was satisfying to come off stage dripping with perspiration and with the crowd cheering.

How I loved our band! And 666 was my closest shot at rock stardom.

The band arose out of the ashes of a previous enterprise. Chris joined us after we had auditioned more than half a dozen bass players. But none of them had the attitude, background, look, equipment and desire of Chris. Tom created original material, sang all the high harmonies, and absolutely tore up the guitar work. I counted myself supremely fortunate to be associated with the talent and desire we had. In addition, I was a wild man on stage. I would dash from one end of the stage to the other, my long black hair streaming out behind me. I often wore stage makeup. Some audiences thought I was a madman. To complete our team, we needed an extraordinary drummer.

That's when Chris brought Charlie into our enterprise.

Needless to say, that weekend was monumental. From the first song, Charlie was a star. He drove the band along like a runaway train. Every song we played was better than I'd ever heard. After the audition, we were all delighted to welcome Charlie to the band. I went home that night as excited as I had ever been. We had a super guitarist, a pounding bass player, and a professional level drummer. Now if I was any good, there should be no stopping us.

I giggled like a schoolboy in his first romantic crush. It was that exciting!

We immediately started practicing five days a week. Not only could Charlie drive the band along, he also learned very quickly. We put together a set of songs, then began working on Tom's originals and an original we had thrown together at one of our earliest practices with Charlie. That song was entitled "Railroads" and would be our first "radio" song.

Practicing five days a week meant that Charlie had to make special arrangements with his part time job, but it also meant that the band was jelling very quickly. We could see that something special was waiting just around the corner, and we were hell-bent to find it.

A solid month of practice with Charlie brought us to the point where we felt we were ready to record. Tom had written many terrific songs but he suggested we record "Railroads", a song we had written together. We went into a home studio one Saturday and spent about four hours recording the music. I would record the vocals a week later, then we all got together to mix the master tape.

I thought the recording came out well and my old friend Mike wanted to get a copy of the record to play on the Cumberland, Maryland rock music radio station. The plan was to use the single to advertise a show the music station would sponsor. That would make us headliners and give us a chance to really let loose in a concert venue.

Tom, Chris, Charlie and I were excited. Promoting a record! How cool is that?

We got a copy of the single to Mike in Cumberland and he set up the gig, working with the local music station.

The gig was scheduled for a Saturday night in late October. The radio station would arrange the venue and provide publicity. Mike would help with the publicity. All we had to do was show up and rock the house!

I immediately headed for Georgetown and the psychedelic clothing stores. I had decided that I needed a pair of leather pants. Jim Morrison of the Doors had made leather pants the coolest item of a rocker's wardrobe and I wanted in!

Unfortunately, the price for actual leather was prohibitive, but I left the shop with a slick pair of tight black satin pants. I grinned all the way home.

The other guys in the group also purchased cool new outfits for the gig.

We practiced every day until we had a concert set that we were happy with. At the time, our public-address system was four "Voice of the Theater" cabinets and a 400-watt amplifier, capable of maiming small animals from half a mile! Chris played bass thru two massive bass cabinets. Tom played guitar thru a mighty Marshall stack with two auxiliary cabinets, and Charlie played the hell out of a dual bass drum kit with amplified drums.

We were loud and exciting. The few times we practiced at my parents' house in Bethesda, children and adults came from blocks away to peer into the basement windows and see what was creating the wall of sound. To this day, my ears still ring.

Our friend Mike had made all the arrangements for the gig. The local radio station was promoting the show, and flyers were distributed at all the local colleges and high schools. I can still remember the thrill when we heard our song being played on the Cumberland radio station!

The equipment filled a rental truck. In addition, I drove my Blazer with two of the massive PA cabinets. It's a long drive from Bethesda to Cumberland so we set out just after noon for the eight o'clock gig. That should give us time to set up, do a quick sound check, then head to the dressing room before the crowd was allowed in.

Now all the clubs and concert venues in and around DC are non-union. We gave it no thought. But Cumberland was a union town, which meant that only union musicians could play there. We had no idea. While we were in our dressing room, the union man came in to ask for our union cards. We stalled him by saying the union cards were in our vehicles. When he left, I grabbed our friend Mike.

"Mike, this guy wants union cards or we can't play."

"Don't worry." Mike replied. "Just keep stalling him off till the end of the gig."

Suddenly, our wonderful plan had a gaping hole. "Just stall him?"

That made no sense. Why hadn't we been informed of this problem some time ago?

"Don't worry." Mike reiterated. "Just rock the house like I know you can."

We grumbled but continued dressing and practicing harmonies.

Ten minutes before the start of the show, the union man reappeared.

"Where's your union cards, boys?"

Now panicked, we made another excuse to get him off our backs. Show time was upon us. Let Mike handle the union man, we've got a show to do.

Just before taking the stage, I pulled the boys around and said.

"Just put everything out of your head except doing a great show, ok?"

"Ok!" Everyone cheered.

We took the stage, replete in our wild new clothes of leather and satin.

We started the show with our radio hit, "Railroads". The crowd screamed and cheered.

Tom finished the song with a burning solo. I leaped into the air and landed with legs spread as we held the thundering crescendo. *When I landed, my new satin pants ripped from crotch to waist!* It's important to add, at this point, that I never wore underwear!

I heard the rip and felt around the back of my new pants to find that I was uncovered.

I dashed off the back of the stage, saying "Do one of Tom's songs till I get back!"

I made for the dressing room and quickly changed my pants. As I left the dressing room, I was accosted by the union man.

Red-faced, he shouted "Union card!".

I was in no mood to deal with him.

"Go to hell!" I shouted back as I went up the stairs and back onto the stage.

Apparently, Mike calmed him down and got rid of him while we played. We didn't see him again.

Despite the torn satin pants, the show went very well.

By the time we wrapped up with "Jailhouse Rock", the crowd was cheering every song. We played "Railroads" as our encore, then left the stage to the crowd stomping out "6!" "6!" "6!".

We came off stage grinning.

"Great show!" Charlie offered.

"Terrific!" Chris echoed.

Tom and I just looked at each other and started to laugh.

"Well, it's certainly been an unusual night." I remarked.

I had no idea how prophetic my words would prove to be.

The show concluded at about 12:20 AM. For the band, there was the prospect of breaking down all the equipment, loading the vehicles, then driving home. The other three boys rode in the rental truck, while I was alone in my Blazer, once again filled to capacity by our PA system.

We patted each other on the back and laughed some more, then left for home. The boys headed for the only available food in town, the donut shop. Now, many of the locals who congregated there were not fans of long hair and the three band members had to talk their way out of a bad situation, I learned later.

For my part, I was headed straight home, but the night had an adventure for me, too.

Cumberland is a mountain town. Mountains can produce thick fog in certain seasons. Fog thick enough that you can barely see the front end of your car. And that's exactly what I encountered.

I had barely rolled out of the downtown section of Cumberland, before I was enveloped in a thick fog.

"Man, I hope this dissipates before I get out on the Interstate."

Unfortunately, it just got worse and I was counting upon the road signs to guide me to the Interstate.

I slowed to a crawl.

"I'm pretty sure the exit to the Interstate was close to here…"

Suddenly, I glimpsed a road sign thru the thick fog.

I quickly followed the sign and within thirty seconds, I was on the Interstate.

Driving thru the mountains can be nerve-wracking in poor visibility conditions. And these were poor visibility conditions. Sudden sharp curves with steep drop-offs are all part of the drive home from Cumberland.

The farther I drove, the worse the conditions became.

Suddenly, a light appeared behind me. I couldn't actually see what it was but it was but I assumed that it was an over-night trucker making his way through the mountains. The trucker, however, was having as much difficulty as I was. As he got closer to my back bumper, I realized that he intended to use me as an extra pair of headlights. He would stay as close to me as possible, knowing that I couldn't get out of his way. This game continued for more than half an hour, while I got more and more anxious. I couldn't speed up to get away and he wouldn't back off. If I slowed, he slowed, all the while he stayed right on my back bumper.

After what felt like hours, we began going downhill and the fog began to dissipate. I shoved down the accelerator pedal and soon the bastard truck was far behind.

The slow pace of travel through the mountains and the lateness of my departure from Cumberland meant that I would arrive back home much later than planned, in fact at dawn.

Bleary-eyed and exhausted, I managed to drag the band equipment out of the Blazer and into my parents' basement, then I collapsed in my bed.

The "Night of 666" was over.

Unfortunately, our record never got enough traction to produce a hit and eventually we split up.

After 666 disbanded, I took a job working in an office of the Federal Government. I was certainly an anomaly in an office setting. My hair was still very long and the word got around quickly. I generated quite a lot of interest among the female employees, since most of the male workers were middle-aged, balding, and pudgy.

Still desirous of rocking, I was approached by a band of younger guys who loved my look and liked my singing. I joined The Rogues out of rock 'n roll desperation. Not that they weren't talented and dedicated, but they wanted to get in a club and play every night. Considering my new day job, that was impossible for me. Also, the fact was that I had no interest in playing other bands' music every night.

So, The Rogues agreed to play my musical choices and look for weekend gigs. To a man, they were very kind in allowing me to make the music selections. That meant that we played a lot of Mott the Hoople songs, David Bowie songs, and other music from other hard rock concert bands. It was during this phase that I began seriously dressing up, including lots of facial makeup. The boys in the band must have been shocked, but were very kind in encouraging me. I remember one repeat gig at an Army base teen club where the elderly lady chaperone came out to the van where we were dressing.

"You boys can play but your singer isn't welcome. He does a lewd show."

I laughed but she was serious. It took explaining that without a singer, there wasn't a show to force her to back down. The kids at the teen club loved us.

Strangely, we played a number of military clubs. The kids loved us.

The Rogues and I created a rock production based upon a story that I wrote. The story revolved around an alien come to Earth. We actually played the entire show, with costumes, at a high school. Surprisingly, it went over well. The audio production was recorded in an audio studio where Jim, the drummer, worked. Once the production was on tape, it was sent to a producer in London. Like so many rock dreams, this one was also doomed.

The Rogues: Jim, Bob, Pat, and Johnny were, and are kind, talented, and generous musicians. But my heart longed for my great love: 666. After about a year with The Rogues, I left the band. I sold my massive Voice of the Theater speaker cabinets, all my microphones, and mic stands. I surrendered to the cruel necessity of making a living, even if it's with the Federal Government. I packed away all my rock outfits and donated both pairs of three-inch-heel stage shoes.

Was it the right thing to do? Absolutely not! When I see a great band like Bad Company, The Ian Hunter Band, or The Rolling Stones, I cry privately for what might have been.

Reviewing gone-by moments of rock magic featuring Mick Ronson, Ian Hunter, David Bowie and all the rest of my favorites makes me realize that we were heroes, as David Bowie declared "for just one day".

I will never willingly surrender those moments of ecstasy on stage, playing to an audience totally in tune with our vibe. I relive those magic moments when everything and everyone was in sync and we believed we would never die and the night would go on forever.

I'm sure heaven has an auditorium with a stage where the rock greats play there every night. They will call us up by name to jam with them.

"We can be heroes for just one day" (But that day could last forever).

In that sense, I dedicate the following to all my former band mates, and especially 666:

The Last Gig: 666

Farewell my brothers! We have trod the Rock 'n
Roll road together for more than ten years. That
road has cracks and pot holes, twists and
tunnels. Some parts lay out in the burning sun
and other parts lead thru dark, cold forests. We
persevered thru the comings and goings of
musical trends and have stayed steadfast in our
core musical beliefs even when others advised us
to change our material and our style. We have
shared much more than dressing rooms and
stages across America. We have shared a dream
and the hard work and dedication that it
requires. Despite long hours, little pay, family
pressures, thieving talent agents, incompetent
management, and the pressures of maintaining a
coherent vision, each of us has stayed focused on
one goal. That goal is to play, write and record
music that we can believe in and be proud of.

How I wish we could have sailed our ship into
that bright harbor of fame and success. But it
was not to be. Our sails suddenly went slack and
the dream we had seen so clearly in the morning
light faded and gradually disappeared when
nighttime overtook us. In the end we simply
stopped believing in that one vision, that one
goal, that single heart beating in four breasts.
The life blood of our enterprise spilled out on the

cold ground and we suddenly walked four separate paths into the future.

Tommy has superior talent. Not only does he play incredibly well, but he writes and sings with heartfelt passion. He is the best guitarist I ever had the joy to work with. He will always be successful and I was lucky as hell to play with him.

Chris is one of the most positive people I have ever worked with. He is an extraordinary bass player. There was never any doubt that he would be asked to join professional bands of top quality. Chris went off to Florida to play on the very active club circuit. It wasn't long before he was picked up by a working band with a record deal. The last I heard from him, the band was touring the US and was slated to go back into the studio.

Charlie...sweet Charlie. Charlie not only had a personality that made him perfect to work with but was the best drummer I know. Despite being short and wiry, Charlie could pound those drums. His playing brought joy to my heart and a smile to my face. And, yes, Charlie was the best drummer I ever worked with.

I was deeply saddened when we broke up. I couldn't think of singing with another band. It is the nature of Rock 'n Roll that bands break apart and new bands form from the pieces. I was fortunate enough to be asked to join a group of younger musicians who were excited about playing and recording. I stayed with them for four years and we recorded an album of songs that made its way to London where a British DJ gave it airplay.

Unfortunately, it was too late for me. 666 was gone and I had already sold my dreams.

My brothers, I wish all the best for each of you and I treasure the time we had together. Your talent, wit and dedication provided me with an experience that few will ever know.

At our last gig, we played well, included our original songs and the audience appreciated our efforts but our hearts weren't in it. At the end of the night, we each packed up our equipment, said goodbye and returned to our separate homes.

The Big Six was gone. I knew that our story, such as it was, would fade. Given time, perhaps it would even fade from our memories. But as I take the time to look back, those were some of the best days of my life.

Fare well, brothers!

CPSIA information can be obtained
at www.ICGtesting.com
Printed in the USA
BVHW040157131218
535537BV00020B/1341/P

9 781725 629196